S0-BAI-919

SIMONE BILES

America's Greatest Gymnast

by Joanne Mattern

Content Consultant

Nanci R. Vargus, Ed.D.
Professor Emeritus, University of Indianapolis

Reading Consultant

Jeanne M. Clidas, Ph.D.
Reading Specialist

Children's Press®
An Imprint of Scholastic Inc.

Library of Congress Cataloging-in-Publication Data

Names: Mattern, Joanne, 1963- author.
Title: Simone Biles: America's Greatest Gymnast/By Joanne Mattern.
Description: New York : Children's Press An Imprint of Scholastic Inc., 2017.
| Series: Rookie Biographies | Includes bibliographical references and index.
Identifiers: LCCN 2016051657| ISBN 9780531232286 (library binding: alk. paper) |
ISBN 9780531238622 (pbk.: alk. paper)
Subjects: LCSH: Biles, Simone, 1997—Juvenile literature. | African American women
gymnasts—Biography—Juvenile literature | Women Olympic athletes—United
States—Biography—Juvenile literature.
Classification: LCC GV460.2.B55 M37 2017 | DDC 796.44092—dc23
LC record available at https://lccn.loc.gov/2016051657

No part of this publication may be reproduced in whole or in part, or stored in a retrieval system,
or transmitted in any form or by any means, electronic, mechanical, photocopying, recording, or
otherwise, without written permission of the publisher. For information regarding permission, write to
Scholastic Inc., Attention: Permissions Department, 557 Broadway, New York, NY 10012.

Produced by Spooky Cheetah Press
Design by Judith Christ-Lafond
Poem by Jodie Shepherd

© 2018 by Scholastic Inc.

All rights reserved. Published in 2018 by Children's Press, an imprint of Scholastic Inc.

Printed in Malaysia 108

SCHOLASTIC, CHILDREN'S PRESS, ROOKIE BIOGRAPHIES™, and associated logos are trademarks
and/or registered trademarks of Scholastic Inc., 557 Broadway, New York, NY 10012.

1 2 3 4 5 6 7 8 9 10 R 27 26 25 24 23 22 21 20 19 18

Photographs ©: cover: Alex Livesey/Getty Images; back cover: David Ramos/Getty Images; 3
background: spawns/iStockphoto; 3 bottom: Kyodo News/Getty Images; 4-5: Alex Livesey/Getty
Images; 6: Leslye Davis/The New York Times/Redux Pictures; 8: Courtesy of the Biles Family; 11: Joe
Scarnici/Getty Images; 12: David J. Phillip/AP Images; 15: David Drufke/ZUMA Press/Newscom; 16:
David Butler/USA Today; 18-19: Virginia Mayo/AP Images; 20: PA Images/Alamy Images; 23: Bryan
Smith/ZUMA Press, Inc./Alamy Images; 24-25: Leon Neal/AFP/Getty Images; 26: Troy Taormina/USA
Today; 29: Michael Ciaglo/Houston Chronicle/AP Images; 30: Cheryle Myers/Dreamstime; 31 top:
Dmitri Lovetsky/AP Images; 31 center top: David Butler/USA Today; 31 center bottom: PA Images/
Alamy Images; 31 bottom: David Drufke/ZUMA Press/Newscom; 32: Cheryle Myers/Dreamstime.

Maps by Mapping Specialists

Sources:
Page 10: Fincher, Julia. "Who Is...Simone Biles?" NBC Sports accessed at http://www.nbcolympics.com/
news/who-simone-biles
Page 13: You make your own luck. You make it in training." The Day accessed at http://theday.co.uk/
sport/you-make-your-own-luck-you-make-it-in-training
Page 14: Fincher, Julia. "Who is... Simone Biles." accessed at www.nbcolympics.com

TABLE OF CONTENTS

Meet Simone Biles

Simone Biles is a world-famous athlete. She has won more medals in gymnastics than any other American. Simone is also an **innovator**. She changed women's gymnastics with her lively, fun **routines**.

Simone Biles was born in Ohio on March 14, 1997. Her mother was not able to take care of her. Simone and her younger sister were adopted by their grandparents. They lived with them in Texas. Simone calls her grandparents Mom and Dad. To her, they are her real parents.

Simone (left) poses with her parents and sister Adria.

CANADA

UNITED
STATES

Columbus ● OHIO

TEXAS
Spring ■

MEXICO

MAP KEY
● City where Simone
Biles was born
■ City where Simone
Biles lives

Area
enlarged

7

Simone's skills were obvious from an early age.

Discovering Gymnastics

Simone always had a lot of energy. She used to do backflips off her family's mailbox!
When Simone was six, she took a school trip to a local gym. She saw older girls doing gymnastics. Little Simone was so excited. She could not just watch! She started to copy the girls' routines.

Simone was invited to join the gym. After a while, she started training with a coach named Aimee Boorman. When Simone was 10 years old, she began **competing** in elite gymnastics. Elite gymnasts train very hard to be the best in the world.

FAST FACT!

Simone said Boorman "is like a second mom to me because she's been there since I was eight years old."

Here is Simone with Coach Boorman.

11

It takes a lot of practice to become a world-class gymnast.

Star Power

At first, Simone went to school like other kids. However, it was hard to go to school and do gymnastics, too. When she was 13, Simone started to be homeschooled. She was able to spend hours every day training in the gym.

FAST FACT!

"Practice creates confidence. You make your own luck. You make it in training."
—Simone Biles

Three years later, Simone competed in an important gymnastics event. It was called the Secret U.S. Classic. Simone had a terrible day. She fell and made mistakes. "I thought it was the end of the world," she said. But Simone did not let this setback stop her.

Simone performs on the balance beam at the Secret U.S. Classic.

That same year, Simone competed at the U.S. **championships**. No one expected her to do well. Simone surprised everyone. She won the all-around gold medal. She also won silver medals on the vault, balance beam, uneven bars, and floor.

Here is Simone on the winner's podium.

Simone showed she was the best in America. Now it was time to take on the world! Gymnasts from around the globe met at the world championships in 2013. Simone outshone them all. She won the all-around title. She won a gold medal for her floor routine. She won a silver on the vault. And she won a bronze on the balance beam.

Simone flies on the uneven bars.

Simone "flips out" during the
2015 world championships.

That same year, Simone invented her own move. The "Biles" is a double flip with a half twist. At the end, Simone lands facing forward. Most flips end with a backward landing. A forward landing is harder because the gymnast cannot see the floor as she spins.

FAST FACT!

Simone won four all-around titles at the world championships between 2013 and 2016. No one had ever done that before!

Golden Dreams

In 2016, Simone was ready for a new challenge. She made the U.S. Olympic team. She and her four teammates would be competing in Rio de Janeiro, Brazil. The team trained hard every day. The gymnasts had to give up a lot of fun things. They could not eat any junk food. They did not have time to spend with their friends.

Teammates (clockwise from top left) Madison Kocian, Gabby Douglas, Aly Raisman, Laurie Hernandez, and Simone Biles pose at the top of the Empire State Building.

Simone led her team to an all-around gold medal. Then she went on to win three more golds.

The world fell in love with Simone. They admired her strength and determination. They loved her sunny smile and her sense of fun.

Simone carries the U.S. flag at the closing ceremony of the 2016 Summer Olympics.

Simone puts her own twist on throwing out the first pitch at a Houston Astros game.

After the Olympics, Simone was glad to have some time off. She was happy to be at home and play with her dogs.

During her time off, Simone made a music video with Jake Miller. She visited the set of *Pretty Little Liars*. That is her favorite TV show. In September 2016, she set off on a 36-city U.S. tour with her Olympic teammates.

Simone is called the best female gymnast of all time. She showed the world that a gymnast can be strong and also have fun. She is a true superstar who inspires others to do their best.

Timeline of Simone Biles's Life

1997 **2003** **2007**

Born on March 14

Begins taking gymnastics lessons

Begins competing as an elite gymnast

Wins the world
championships
all-around event

Wins five medals
at the Olympics

2013 > **2014** > **2015** > **2016**

ns the U.S. and
·ld championships
around events

Becomes the first woman
to win a third straight
world championship in
the all-around

A Poem About Simone Biles

She twists and twirls and leaps and jumps,
and always with bright smiles.
She makes it look so easy—
Olympian Simone Biles!

You Can Be a Champion

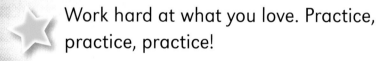
Work hard at what you love. Practice, practice, practice!

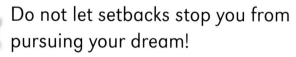
Do not let setbacks stop you from pursuing your dream!

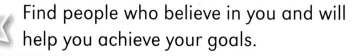
Find people who believe in you and will help you achieve your goals.

Glossary

championships (CHAM-pee-uhn-ships): contests that determine which team or player will be the overall winner

competing (kuhm-PEET-ing): trying hard to outdo others at a task, race, or contest

innovator (in-uh-VAY-tur): someone who introduces new ideas or inventions

routines (roo-TEENS): series or combination of movements that make up a performance

Index

Facts for Now

Visit this Scholastic Web site for more information on Simone Biles
and download the Teaching Guide for this series:

www.factsfornow.scholastic.com

Enter the keywords Simone Biles

About the Author

Joanne Mattern has written more than 250 books for children.
She especially likes writing biographies because she loves to learn about
real people and the things they do. Joanne also enjoys watching many
different sports, although she is not very good at playing them! She grew up
in New York State and still lives there with her husband, four children, and
several pets.